Easy-to-Make
Elegant Jewelry

Easy-to-Make
Elegant Jewelry
CHIC PROJECTS THAT SPARKLE & SHINE

DESIGN ORIGINALS
an Imprint of Fox Chapel Publishing
www.d-originals.com

W e would like to acknowledge the extremely talented creative team at Cousin Corporation of America for their contributions to this book. A special thanks to Kristine Regan Daniel, Jennifer Eno-Wolf, and Chloe Pemberton for their additional support.

Acquisition editor: Peg Couch
Cover and page designers: Llara Pazdan & Justin Speers
Layout designer: Wendy Reynolds
Editors: Colleen Dorsey & Katie Weeber
Technical editor: Melissa Younger
Copy editor: Laura Taylor
Photography: Mike Mihalo
Photography styling: Llara Pazdan & Kati Erney

ISBN 978-1-4972-0311-2

© 2017 by Cousin Corporation of America and New Design Originals Corporation, *www.d-originals.com*, an imprint of Fox Chapel Publishing, 800-457-9112, 1970 Broad Street, East Petersburg, PA 17520.

Library of Congress Cataloging-in-Publication Data

Names: Daniel, Kristine Regan, author.
Title: Easy-to-make elegant jewelry / Kristine Regan Daniel.
Description: East Petersburg : Design Originals, [2017] | Includes index.
Identifiers: LCCN 2017006732 | ISBN 9781497203112 (pbk.)
Subjects: LCSH: Jewelry making.
Classification: LCC TT212 .D35 2017 | DDC 745.594/2--dc23
LC record available at https://lccn.loc.gov/2017006732

Printed in the United States of America
First printing

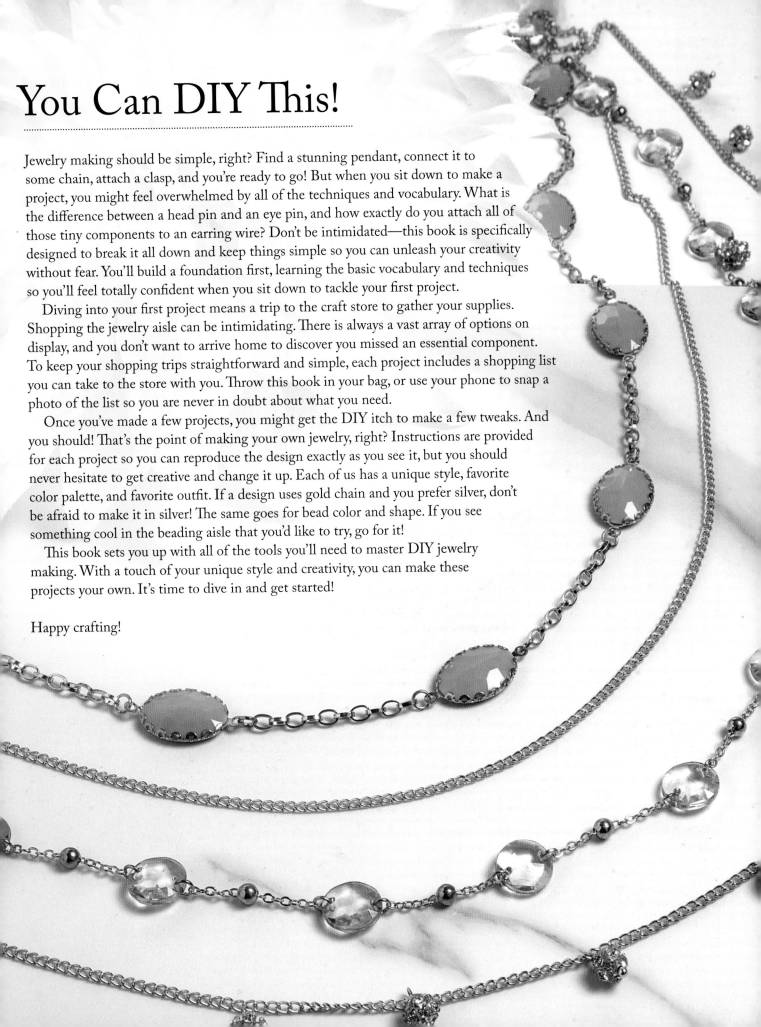

You Can DIY This!

Jewelry making should be simple, right? Find a stunning pendant, connect it to some chain, attach a clasp, and you're ready to go! But when you sit down to make a project, you might feel overwhelmed by all of the techniques and vocabulary. What is the difference between a head pin and an eye pin, and how exactly do you attach all of those tiny components to an earring wire? Don't be intimidated—this book is specifically designed to break it all down and keep things simple so you can unleash your creativity without fear. You'll build a foundation first, learning the basic vocabulary and techniques so you'll feel totally confident when you sit down to tackle your first project.

Diving into your first project means a trip to the craft store to gather your supplies. Shopping the jewelry aisle can be intimidating. There is always a vast array of options on display, and you don't want to arrive home to discover you missed an essential component. To keep your shopping trips straightforward and simple, each project includes a shopping list you can take to the store with you. Throw this book in your bag, or use your phone to snap a photo of the list so you are never in doubt about what you need.

Once you've made a few projects, you might get the DIY itch to make a few tweaks. And you should! That's the point of making your own jewelry, right? Instructions are provided for each project so you can reproduce the design exactly as you see it, but you should never hesitate to get creative and change it up. Each of us has a unique style, favorite color palette, and favorite outfit. If a design uses gold chain and you prefer silver, don't be afraid to make it in silver! The same goes for bead color and shape. If you see something cool in the beading aisle that you'd like to try, go for it!

This book sets you up with all of the tools you'll need to master DIY jewelry making. With a touch of your unique style and creativity, you can make these projects your own. It's time to dive in and get started!

Happy crafting!

Contents

24

Chandelier Teardrop
Earrings

26

Champagne Bubbles
Bracelet

28

Gold Spike
Earrings

30

Twisted Wire
Gemstone Cuff

32

Dazzle Bling
Ring

34

Summer Breeze
Dangle Earrings

36

Pearl Beaded
Cuff Bracelet

38

Seafoam Silver Chain
Necklace

40

Champagne Woven
Earrings

42

Frosted Crystal
Necklace

44

Beaded Tassel
Bracelet Set

46

Coral Swirl
Earrings

48

Lariat Layers
Necklace Set

50

Silver Bubbles
Earrings

52

Evening Elegance
Necklace

54

Clear Skies Beaded
Earrings

56

Starlight Shimmer
Necklace

58

Gold Leaf Chain
Earrings

60

Chain-Link Crystal
Bracelet

62

Gold Wrap Crystal
Earrings

Getting Started

If you are totally new to jewelry making, this is the place to start.
This section will help you build a foundation by allowing you to familiarize
yourself with the common tools and materials used in jewelry making.
You'll also find step-by-step tutorials for the techniques you'll need to assemble
the projects in this book. When you're finished, you'll be able to spot cable
chain when shopping at the craft store and be able to execute a flawless
wire wrap. Once you have a grasp of the content in this section,
you'll be ready to tackle your first jewelry project!

Tools

You don't need to spend a lot of money purchasing a vast array of tools to get started with jewelry making. A few sets of pliers and a handful of extras will allow you to make all of the projects in this book. Here are the common tools of jewelry making.

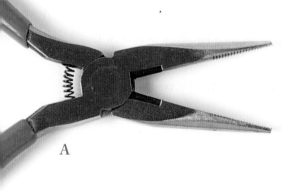

A

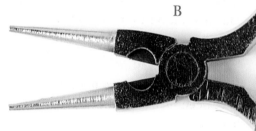

B

C

D

THE ESSENTIALS

Needle-nose pliers (A) come to a tapered point, making them the perfect tool to get into small areas of a jewelry design. Use this tool to hold small pieces, open and close jump rings, and manipulate wire.

Round-nose pliers (B) have rounded prongs that are used for making loops in wire, head pins, or eye pins.

Crimping pliers (C) are pliers made specifically for use with crimp tubes. The specially shaped grooves in these pliers will attach a crimp tube to beading wire in the most secure way possible.

Wire cutters (D) should always be used to cut jewelry wire—do not use scissors. Regular wire cutters that you get from the hardware store will work, but flush cutters made specifically for jewelry making are recommended.

THE EXTRAS

Memory wire cutters are heavy-duty wire cutters made specifically to cut the coils of memory wire without affecting their shape.

E-6000® glue is an extra-strong craft glue. It is perfect for securing cord ends or connecting other components.

A *jewelry hammer* is a lightweight hammer used for shaping metal. This hammer has two heads—a flat head and a round head.

A *ring mandrel* is a tapered rod used to measure the size of a ring or, in the case of jewelry making, to shape a ring to a specific size.

Beading tweezers are helpful when it comes to sorting and handling beads. Their extra-fine tip means they can pick up tiny beads more easily than your fingers can. Some tweezers come with a small, spoon-like scoop on the back end for easily collecting loose beads.

A *bead reamer* is like a mini drill that comes with an assortment of tips, which are used like drill bits. The tips can clean up the edges of a hole drilled in a bead, straighten the hole, or otherwise enlarge or re-shape the hole.

Awls are sharp, pointed tools used for making holes in leather.

Beads

Of course beads are needed for jewelry making, but you might be surprised by the vast number of shapes and sizes that are available. What is the difference between a rondelle and a briolette? Take a look at this collection of commonly used beads to learn some important terms.

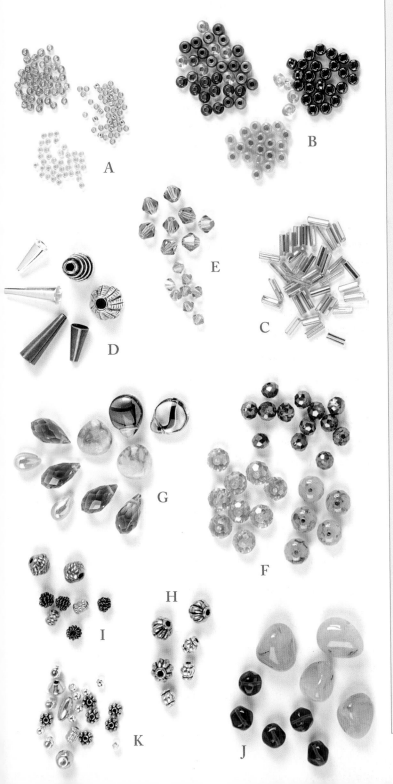

Seed beads (A) are extra-small beads, ranging in size from about 1.5mm to 3mm. Their sizes are listed as a number over zero (15/0, 12/0, etc.). The smaller the initial number, the larger the bead.

E–beads (B) are large seed beads, size 6/0, or about 4mm.

Bugle beads (C) are small, tube-shaped beads.

Cones (D) have a cone shape with a wide base at one end and a tapered point at the other. They are hollow, so they can fit over small components in a design.

Bicones (E) look like two cones that have been joined at the bottom. In profile, they have a diamond shape, with the widest point across the center and a tapered point at each end.

Rondelles (F) look like round, spherical beads that have been squashed just slightly. They look a bit like inner tubes.

Briolettes (G) have a teardrop or pear shape. They are almost always faceted (cut to have multiple faces, like a diamond) and always side-drilled, with a hole through the tapered point of the bead, rather than through the center of the bead.

Melon beads (H) actually have a pumpkin-like appearance, with raised, rounded sections running from top to bottom.

Beehive beads (I) are shaped like beehives you might see in cartoons with raised, rounded sections like rings running around the circumference of the bead.

Nuggets (J) have no specific shape. They are like pebbles you might pick up on the beach—random and unique.

Spacer beads (K) refer to small, plain, typically metallic beads. These beads serve an important function by adding space to a jewelry design without detracting from the focal beads.

Stringing Materials

Stringing materials include all of the items you can string beads onto or attach beads to. Stringing materials like cotton rope or hemp cord can also be used without beads to create jewelry using decorative knotwork. Here is a collection of common stringing materials.

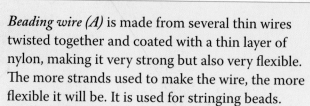

Beading wire (A) is made from several thin wires twisted together and coated with a thin layer of nylon, making it very strong but also very flexible. The more strands used to make the wire, the more flexible it will be. It is used for stringing beads.

Gauge wire (B) is a single piece of metal measured by the thickness of its diameter (gauge). The smaller the gauge number, the thicker the wire is. Gauge wire has varying flexibility and can be used for stringing beads, wire wrapping, or creating fixed components in a design.

Memory wire (C) is gauge wire that has been shaped into coils. The coils can be cut or stretched, but cannot be used for wrapping or other decorative wire work.

Cord (D) generally encompasses any non-wire material used for stringing beads. It is typically made of fabric, fiber, or natural materials. Cording includes satin, leather or suede, rope, or hemp.

Monofilament (E) is an often transparent synthetic cord, similar to fishing line. It is available in different strengths based on the amount of weight it can hold (2 lb. monofilament can hold two pounds of beads).

Chain (F) is a series of metal links joined together. The links may be closed (solid pieces of metal) or open (with a slit cut through them so they can be opened and removed from the main chain). Chain is available in a variety of shapes—cable, curb, and flat-link are the types you'll encounter the most in this book. (For more about different kinds of chain, see the glossary.)

TOOLS & MATERIALS

Findings

Findings are all of the components used to build a piece of jewelry. They attach, link, and hold together all of the elements in a design. Here is a collection of common jewelry findings.

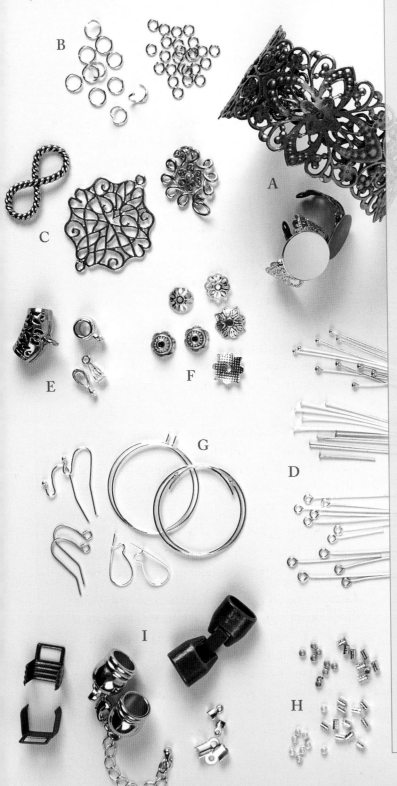

Bases (A) are unembellished blanks that you build upon to create a jewelry piece, such as a ring blank or a bangle bracelet blank.

Jump rings (B) are the most commonly used component to connect different pieces in a jewelry design. They are almost always "open" with a slit cut into the ring so it can be opened and closed. They are also available as solid rings, called closed jump rings.

Connectors (C) are bars, beads, or other components that have a loop (or loops) on each end. They are used to connect separate elements in a design.

Head pins, ball head pins, and *eye pins (D)* are short lengths of wire finished at one end with a flat head (head pin), ball (ball head pin), or loop (eye pin). Beads are strung onto the pins and the ends are formed into loops to create decorative bead drops or links.

Bails (E) are used to attach pendants to chain, cord, wire, or other stringing materials.

Bead caps (F) are bowl-shaped decorative components paired with beads. Their shape allows them to fit snugly against the bead as if they were part of it rather than a separate element.

Earring wires (G) encompass any component used to hook an earring to the ear. They come in a variety of shapes including hooks (also known as earring wires or French hooks), kidney wires, and hoops.

Crimp tubes and *crimp beads (H)* are used to finish the ends of beading wire.

Cord ends (I) are used to finish the ends of cord designs without knots. They come as caps that slide over the cord ends and are secured with glue, or crimps, which are clamped onto the cord ends.

Clasps (J, at top) are placed at the ends of a design and are used to close it. They come in numerous shapes and sizes including lobster clasps, toggle sets, or magnetic clasps.

Opening and Closing Jump Rings

Jump rings are used to connect different jewelry components to one another. Opening and closing a jump ring incorrectly can affect its shape or leave gaps that might allow jewelry components to fall off, so it's important to know how to do it properly.

> Project(s) using this technique appear on pages 24, 26, 32, 34, 38, 42, 44, 48, 50, 52, 54, 56, 60, and 62.

1 *Position the pliers.* It is best to use two needle-nose pliers for this process. Using the pliers, grasp the ring on each side of the opening.

2 *Start twisting the ring open.* To keep the ring's shape, it should be twisted open, with the ends moving back to front instead of side to side. To do this, twist one wrist toward your body and the other wrist away from your body.

3 *Finish opening the ring.* Continue twisting until the opening is wide enough to attach the desired components. String on components like chain, clasps, or bead drops.

4 *Close the ring.* Following the method in Steps 1–3, reposition the pliers and twist the ring closed. If there is a gap, gently wiggle the pliers, moving the ends of the ring backward and forward while gently pressing them together. The ends should slightly overlap and then snap together tightly so the tension of the metal will hold the ring closed.

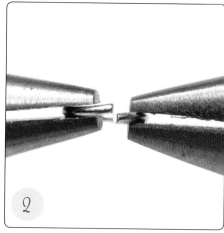

Split rings are like miniature key rings. They are made of coiled wire and do not have openings like jump rings, making them a more secure and sturdy option for heavy components. To attach items to a split ring, use a head pin or eye pin to hold the coils open.

Attaching Crimp Tubes/Beads

Crimp tubes and beads are used with beading wire and secured using crimping pliers. Once crimped, the tubes/beads stay in place on the wire, so they can be used to attach clasps or hold individual beads or groups of beads in a certain place.

Project(s) using this technique appear on pages 36, 40, 42, 44, and 60.

1 *String the clasp.* String a crimp tube and a clasp (such as one half of a toggle clasp or a single lobster clasp) onto a strand of beading wire. Bring the end of the wire back through the crimp tube, creating a ½" (1.3cm) tail. Push the crimp tube up the wire so it is close to the clasp.

2 *Make the first crimp.* Place the crimp tube in the U-shaped groove of the crimping pliers (closest to the handles). Separate the wires in the crimp tube so they are parallel and do not cross. Firmly collapse the crimp tube, forming it into a U shape with one wire in each groove.

3 *Make the second crimp.* Place the crimp tube in the oval-shaped groove of the crimping pliers (farthest from the handles). Position the crimp tube so the U shape is sideways. Squeeze the pliers so the ends of the U shape come together.

4 *Check the wire.* Once crimped, the tube will look like this. Tug on the wire to be sure it is secure. The tail of the wire can be hidden in beads strung onto the wire.

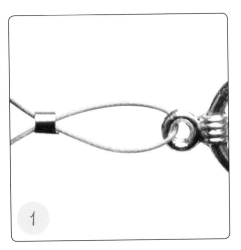

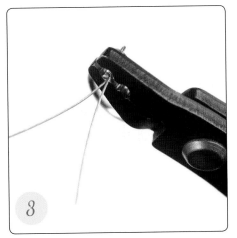

Crimp beads (below right) can be shaped using the crimp tube method described above. They are formed into smooth cylinders using the oval-shaped groove of the crimping pliers, or simply flattened using needle-nose pliers.

Cutting Chain

Jewelry projects often require lengths of chain that are shorter than what you can purchase. Use wire cutters to cut closed-link chain to the length needed. This method allows you to easily cut multiple pieces of chain to the same length without measuring each piece.

Project(s) using this technique appear on pages 34, 38, 44, 52, 56, and 58.

1 *Cut the first length.* Measure the length of chain needed and use wire cutters to cut it off the original chain. Remember, the cut link will fall off, so do not include this in the measurement.

2 *Cut the remaining lengths.* Thread a head pin through an end link of the cut chain, then through an end link of the original chain. Line up the chain links, and cut the next length of chain to match the first. Repeat to cut the remaining pieces needed.

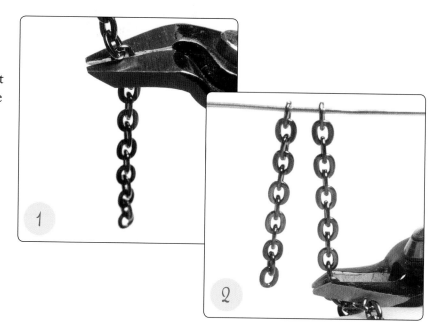

Open-Link Chain

Open chain links can be opened and closed just like jump rings (see page 14). Instead of cutting open-link chain, you can open and close the links to separate the necessary lengths of chain.

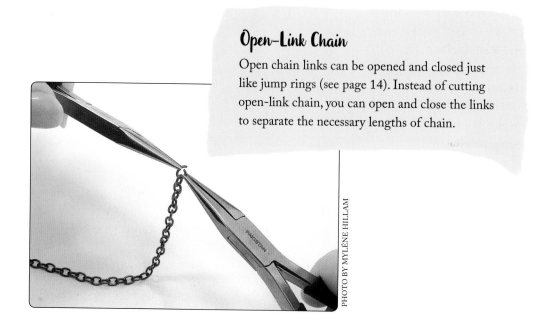

PHOTO BY MYLÈNE HILLAM

Forming a Loop

Round-nose pliers can be used to make loops in head pins, eye pins, or beading wire. Loops allow the pin or wire to be attached to other items using jump rings or other loops. Here's how to make a loop in an eye pin to create a bead link.

> Project(s) using this technique appear on pages 24, 28, 32, 38, 42, 44, 52, and 58.

1. *Trim the pin.* Slide a bead (or beads) onto an eye pin. Using needle-nose pliers, bend the tail of the eye pin to form a right angle with the bead(s). Trim the tail about ¼" (0.5cm) beyond the last bead.

2. *Start forming the loop.* Grasp the end of the wire with round-nose pliers. Rotate your wrist to wrap the wire around the pliers, forming a loop. The jaws of the pliers taper, so the size of the loop can be adjusted based on its position in the pliers.

3. *Finish forming the loop.* You may need to release the pin, reposition the pliers, and rotate them again to completely close the loop.

4. *Check the finished link.* When finished, there will be a loop on each side of the bead so other components can be attached to each side.

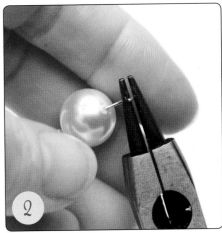
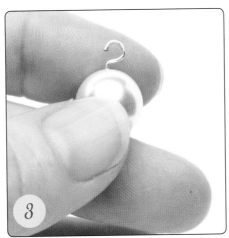
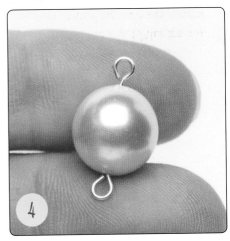

Tip: If you have trouble forming a loop at the end of a 1" (2.5cm) eye pin or head pin, you can always use a 2" (5cm) pin instead and simply trim off the excess.

Tip: You can convert a head pin to an eye pin by trimming off the flat head and forming a loop on that end instead.

Forming a Wrapped Loop

A wrapped loop is stronger than a basic loop, making it perfect for connecting heavy jewelry components. It also adds a decorative touch.

Project(s) using this technique appear on pages 34, 38, 48, 54, 58, 60, and 62.

1 **Bend the pin.** Slide a bead (or beads) onto a head pin. Grasp the head pin with round-nose pliers, resting the pliers against the top of the bead. Bend the tail of the pin to form a right angle with the bead(s).

2 **Start forming the loop.** Reposition the pliers so one prong is below the bend in the wire and one prong is above it. Wrap the tail of the head pin around the top prong, forming a loop.

3 **Finish forming the loop.** Reposition the pliers so the bottom prong is in the loop formed in Step 2. Finish forming the loop by wrapping the tail of the head pin around the bottom prong.

4 **Make the wrap.** Holding the loop with the pliers, wrap the tail of the head pin around the stem of the loop from the bottom of the loop to the top of the bead(s). Once the wrap is complete, trim away any excess from the tail of the head pin.

5 **Secure the tail.** Use needle-nose pliers or crimping pliers to tuck the trimmed tail into the wrap.

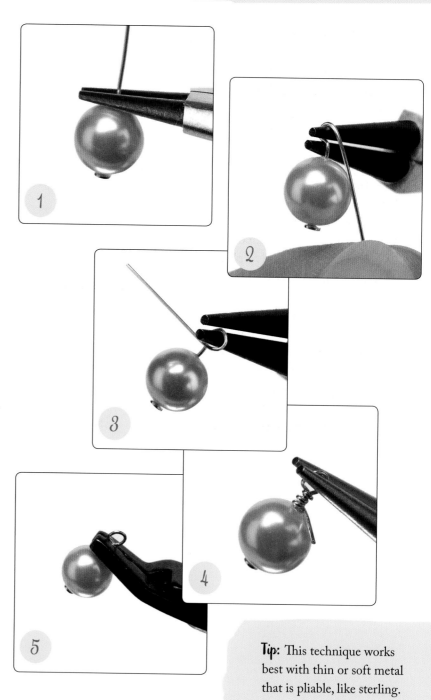

Tip: This technique works best with thin or soft metal that is pliable, like sterling.

Forming Wire Wraps with Beads

With this technique, you can use wire to wrap beads securely around any charm or finding. Simply thread beads on as you go, following the instructions below.

Project(s) using this technique appear on page 46.

1 **Attach the wire.** Cut a length of wire long enough to complete the desired wrap. Secure one end of the wire to the base component by wrapping it around the base three times.

2 **Add the first bead.** String a bead onto the wire, positioning the bead against the base. On the other side of the bead, wrap the wire around the base component twice to secure the bead in place. Then slide on another bead.

3 **Finish.** Repeat Step 2 until the desired number of beads has been added. Finish by wrapping the wire around the base component three times. Trim away any excess wire and use pliers to flatten the wire tail and loops snugly against the base.

Wrapping Beads with Wire

A wire wrap is a beautiful effect to add to a bead. The technique works best on teardrop or pear-shaped beads and can be used to create embellished bead drops, pendants, or earrings.

Project(s) using this technique appear on pages 48 and 62.

1 *String the bead.* String a bead onto a length of wire. Center the bead along the wire, then bend the wire up at each side of the bead. Smooth the ends of the wire up along the sides of the bead so they meet at the top.

2 *Make the loop.* Use round-nose pliers to form a loop at the top of the bead. Refer to Steps 1–3 for Forming a Wrapped Loop on page 18.

3 *Form the wrap.* Holding the loop with the pliers, wrap the tail of the wire around the stem of the loop and around the top of the bead.

4 *Trim and finish.* Continue the wrap to the desired position on the bead. Once the wrap is complete, trim away any excess wire and use needle-nose pliers to tuck the tail into the wrap.

1

2

3

4

Ready, Set, Craft!

The earrings shown here use the technique
Attaching Crimp Tubes/Beads, and the bracelet is
so simple that you don't need any of the techniques!
Go to pages 30 and 40 to make these pieces now,
or just turn the page to get started with all of
the stunning projects in this book!

Step-by-Step Projects

Now that you know the lingo and understand the basic techniques, it's time to put what you've learned into practice and make some projects. Remember to use the shopping lists to help navigate the jewelry section at the store. And don't be afraid to choose chain, beads, and colors that suit your personal taste to make a project your own!

Level:

Time:

The "Level" for each project indicates whether it is Beginner, Intermediate, or Advanced.

The "Time" for each project indicates how long each project will take, not including glue drying time. One diamond means less than an hour; two diamonds means between one and two hours; and three diamonds means more than two hours.

Chandelier Teardrop Earrings

Pearls, teardrop pendants, and stylized filigree connectors come together in these earrings to create an upscale, elegant look. Set these aside for a special occasion and pair them with other pearl, glass bead, or silver jewelry pieces.

1 *Make the center drop.* Slide a bicone, a pearl, and a bicone onto an eye pin and form a loop. Connect the top loop of this bead link to the middle loop on the bottom of a chandelier connector. Use a 4mm jump ring to connect the bottom loop of this bead link to the top loop of a teardrop.

2 *Make the outer bead drops.* Slide a bicone, a white pearl, a bicone, a white pearl, a bicone, and a white pearl onto a head pin and form a loop. Connect the loop of this bead drop to the left bottom loop on the chandelier connector. Repeat to make and connect an identical bead drop to the right side of the chandelier connector.

3 *Make the final bead drops.* Slide a bicone, a white pearl, a bicone, a white pearl, and a bicone onto a head pin and form a loop. Use a 4mm jump ring to connect this bead drop between the outer left bead drop and the center drop. Repeat to make and connect an identical bead drop between the outer right bead drop and the center drop.

4 *Connect the connectors.* Slide a white pearl onto an eye pin and form a loop. Use the loops on each end of this bead link to connect the top loop of the chandelier connector to the bottom of a filigree connector.

5 *Add the earring wire.* Open the loop of an earring wire and attach it to the top of the filigree connector.

6 *Make the other earring.* Repeat Steps 1–5 for the matching earring.

SHOPPING LIST

- 2 - 17 x 16mm teardrops (silver/clear)
- 24 - 4mm glass round beads (white pearl)
- 28 - 4mm crystal bicone beads (clear)
- 2 - 24 x 12mm filigree connectors (gunmetal)
- 2 - 11 x 25mm 3-loop chandelier connectors (gunmetal)
- 8 - 2" (5cm) head pins (silver)
- 4 - 1" (2.5cm) eye pins (silver)
- 6 - 4mm jump rings (silver)
- 2 - Earring wires (silver)

TOOLS

- Needle-nose pliers
- Round-nose pliers
- Wire cutters

TECHNIQUES

- Opening and Closing Jump Rings
- Forming a Loop

Level:
◆ ● ●

Time:
◆ ● ●

Champagne Bubbles Bracelet

The coastal look of this bracelet goes well with white dress shorts or capris. It's also an understated piece to pair with a work outfit. The neutral color will work with any bright top you have in your summer wardrobe.

1 *Cut the cord.* Measure the desired total bracelet length and subtract 1" (2.5cm) for the clasp, or however large your clasp is. Double that number and cut a piece of cotton rope cord to that length (this one was 13" [33cm]). Fold the rope cord in half.

2 *Wrap the beaded cord.* Use tape to secure one end of the 40" (105cm) beaded cord to the fold of the rope cord. Wrap the beaded cord around the entire length of the folded rope cord, completely covering it.

3 *Finish the cords.* Use tape to secure the ends of the beaded cord to the ends of the rope cord. Trim the ends so they are even, leaving the tape in place.

4 *Attach the cord ends.* Apply glue to the inside of each cord end. Push one end of the joined cords into each cord end and allow the glue to dry.

5 *Add the clasp.* Use the jump ring to connect the lobster clasp to the loop of one cord end.

 SHOPPING LIST

- 18" (46cm) - 3mm cotton rope cord (coral)
- 40" (105cm) - 5mm nylon & glass beaded cord (cream)
- 2 - 12 x 20mm cord ends (silver)
- 1 - 8mm jump ring (silver)
- 1 - Large decorative lobster clasp (silver)

TOOLS

- Scissors
- Tape
- Craft glue

TECHNIQUES

- Opening and Closing Jump Rings

Gold Spike Earrings

Get that edgy look with these cool spike earrings. They'll add some attitude to any outfit without being over the top. If you're feeling extra adventurous, pair them with bold eye makeup and a choker.

Level:
◆ ● ●

Time:
◆ ● ●

1 *Prepare the wire.* Cut a 1¾" (4.5cm) length of wire. Curve the wire into the same half circle shape as a curved connector.

2 *Add the spikes.* String 5 spikes onto the wire. Form a loop at each end of the wire, connecting the loops to the bottom loops of a curved connector.

3 *Add the earring wire.* Connect the loop of the earring wire to the top loop of the curved connector.

4 *Make the other earring.* Repeat Steps 1–3 for the matching earring.

SHOPPING LIST

- 10 - 34 x 5mm spikes (matte gold)
- 2 - 21mm curved connectors (gold)
- 3½" (9cm) - 20-gauge wire (gold)
- 2 - Earring wires (gold)

TOOLS

- Round-nose pliers
- Wire cutters

TECHNIQUES

- Forming a Loop

Twisted Wire Gemstone Cuff

Level:
♦ ● ●

Time:
♦ ● ●

This design is the perfect piece to show off in the summer with a pair of gold sunglasses. It also looks great with a three-quarter-sleeve jacket. Have fun shopping for the focal gemstone and creating the twists and turns in the wire wrapping.

1 *Attach the gemstone and wire.* Cut a 36" (92cm) length of wire. Place one end of the wire underneath the gemstone slice and use adhesive to adhere the gemstone slice and wire end to the top center of the cuff. Allow the adhesive to dry thoroughly—overnight is best, but a few hours should do the trick.

2 *Wrap the base.* Wrap the protruding wire multiple times underneath and around the base of the gemstone, parallel to the cuff.

3 *Wrap the gemstone.* Bring the wire up over the gemstone, across to the other side, and back under and around the cuff, keeping the wire snug to the gemstone. Repeat about 7 more times, weaving the leading wire through the wrapped wire wherever possible for added security.

4 *Finish wrapping.* Tuck the end of the wire under the gemstone again. Apply additional adhesive to hold the wire in place. Allow the adhesive to dry thoroughly.

5 *Adjust the wire.* Use round-nose pliers to make decorative twists in the wires crossing the top of the gemstone to further tighten the wire against the gemstone.

SHOPPING LIST

- 1 - 48 x 30mm agate gemstone slice (green)
- 36" (92cm) - 24-gauge wire (gold)
- 1 - Cuff bracelet base (gold)

TOOLS

- Needle-nose pliers
- Round-nose pliers
- Wire cutters
- E-6000® glue

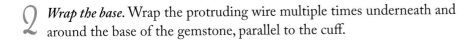

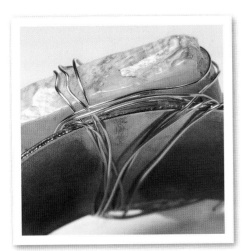

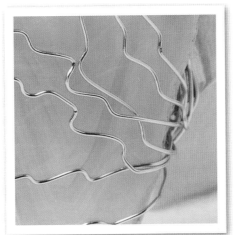

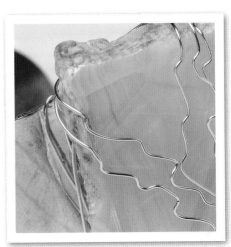

Level:
💎 ● ●

Time:
💎 ● ●

Dazzle Bling Ring

This ring screams party, so make sure you have it on your finger the next time you go out dancing! With its neutral colors, it will pair well with any outfit in your wardrobe—especially a sparkly top.

1 *Make the bead drops.* Slide a bicone onto a head pin and form a loop to make a bead drop. Make a total of 60 bead drops.

2 *Add one cluster.* Slide the loop of 6 bead drops onto a jump ring and connect the jump ring to 1 of the loops on the ring base.

3 *Finish the ring.* Repeat Step 2 for all remaining bead drops, jump rings, and loops of the ring base.

 SHOPPING LIST

- 60 - 4mm glass bicone beads
  (AB champagne/gold)
- 60 - 1" (2.5cm) head pins (silver)
- 10 - 4mm jump rings (silver)
- 1 - Adjustable size 10-loop cluster
  ring base (silver)

TOOLS

- Needle-nose pliers
- Round-nose pliers
- Wire cutters

TECHNIQUES

- Opening and Closing Jump Rings
- Forming a Loop

Summer Breeze Dangle Earrings

These earrings are light, bright, and airy and a perfect fit for your summer wardrobe. They'll look great with a tank top or t-shirt and your favorite shorts. Wear them with coordinating pieces like a teal clutch or a chunky, bright green bangle.

1 **Add the chains.** Cut chains into the lengths shown in the illustration. Attach a jump ring to one end of each length of chain and slide the jump rings onto the earring hoop in the order shown in the illustration. Close the earring hoop.

2 **Create the bead drops.** Slide each bicone onto a separate head pin and form wrapped loops, connecting each bead drop to the end of each length of chain as shown in the illustration.

3 **Add the earring wire.** Attach the loop of an earring wire to the top of the earring hoop.

4 **Make the other earring.** Repeat Steps 1–3 for the matching earring.

SHOPPING LIST

- 18 - 4mm crystal bicone beads (teal green)
- 12 - 4mm crystal bicone beads (lime)
- 8 - 4mm crystal bicone beads (clear)
- 36" (92cm) - 2.3mm cable chain (silver)
- 38 - 1" (2.5cm) head pins (silver)
- 38 - 4mm jump rings (silver)
- 2 - 20mm earring hoops (silver)
- 2 - Earring wires (silver)

TOOLS

- Needle-nose pliers
- Round-nose pliers
- Wire cutters

TECHNIQUES

- Opening and Closing Jump Rings
- Cutting Chain
- Forming a Wrapped Loop

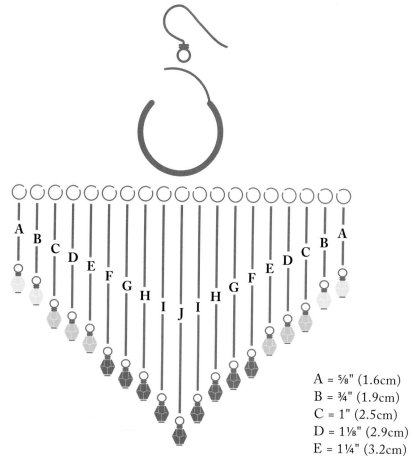

A = ⅝" (1.6cm)	F = 1½" (3.8cm)
B = ¾" (1.9cm)	G = 1⅝" (4.1cm)
C = 1" (2.5cm)	H = 1¾" (4.5cm)
D = 1⅛" (2.9cm)	I = 2" (5.1cm)
E = 1¼" (3.2cm)	J = 2¼" (5.7cm)

Pearl Beaded Cuff Bracelet

Level: 💎 ● ●

Time: 💎 ● ●

This beautiful statement piece will make a splash without overwhelming your outfit. Try it with a cocktail dress paired with a matching pearl necklace and pearl or rhinestone earrings.

1   *Prepare the wire.* Cut nine 12" (31cm) lengths of beading wire. Use crimp tubes to connect one end of each beading wire to the loops on one side of the magnetic clasp.

2   *String five of the strands.* String the following onto every other length of wire (5 strands in total): 1 pearl and 1 rondelle. Then string the following pattern onto these 5 strands a total of 9 times: 3 pearls and 1 rondelle. Finish each of the 5 strands with 1 pearl. Use a crimp tube to connect the other end of each wire to the corresponding loop on the other side of the magnetic clasp.

3   *String four of the strands.* String the following onto the remaining 4 lengths of wire: 2 pearls and 1 rondelle. Then string the following pattern onto these 4 strands a total of 8 times: 3 pearls and 1 rondelle. Finish each of the 4 strands with 3 pearls. Use a crimp tube to connect the other end of each wire to the corresponding loop on the other side of the magnetic clasp.

 SHOPPING LIST

- 261 - 6mm glass round beads (ecru pearl)
- 86 - 4 x 8mm rhinestone rondelle spacer beads (silver)
- 9' (280cm) - Beading wire (silver)
- 18 - Crimp tubes (silver)
- 1 - 56 x 8mm 9-strand magnetic clasp set (silver)

TOOLS

- Crimping pliers
- Wire cutters

TECHNIQUES

- Attaching Crimp Tubes/Beads

Seafoam Silver Chain Necklace

This light, simple necklace is an excellent year-round piece, but it's especially appropriate for summer. This design will pair beautifully with a business casual outfit for work and look just as good with capris and flip-flops for a spontaneous night out.

1 *Start the pendant.* Cut seven 1½" (3.8cm) lengths of chain. Open the loop of one 1" (2.5cm) eye pin and attach 5 of the lengths of chain. Attach the remaining 2 lengths to a 4mm jump ring. Slide the jump ring over the shaft of the eye pin. Slide the silver bead cone onto the eye pin and form a coiled loop at the top. This is done by wrapping the end of the eye pin around the round-nose pliers 3 times to form a small coil. Cut off any excess.

2 *Finish the pendant.* Slide the large barrel bead onto the large eye pin and form a wrapped loop, connecting the 8mm closed jump ring to the loop. Connect the other loop of the beaded eye pin to the eye pin loop at the top of the bead cone from Step 1 to form the completed pendant.

3 *Make the bead links.* Slide a round bead onto each of the remaining eye pins. Form a loop at the end of each eye pin to create 6 bead links.

4 *Connect the links and chain.* Cut one 16" (41cm) length of chain, four 4" (10cm) lengths of chain, and two 3½" (9cm) lengths of chain. Connect the 6 bead links from Step 3 and the 7 lengths of chain in the following order: one 3½" (9cm) chain, one bead link, one 4" (10cm) chain, one bead link, one 4" (10cm) chain, one bead link, one 16" (41cm) chain, one bead link, one 4" (10cm) chain, one bead link, one 4" (10cm) chain, one bead link, and one 3½" (9cm) chain.

5 *Finish the necklace.* Connect each end of the completed chain from Step 4 to the 8mm closed jump ring with the pendant attached.

SHOPPING LIST

- 1 - Large barrel bead (amazonite)
- 6 - 6mm round beads (amazonite)
- 1 - 10mm bead cone (silver)
- 55" (140cm) - 2 x 3mm oval open-link cable chain (silver)
- 7 - 1" (2.5cm) eye pins (silver)
- 1 - 3" (7.5cm) eye pin (silver)
- 1 - 8mm closed jump ring (silver)
- 1 - 4mm jump ring (silver)

TOOLS

- Needle-nose pliers
- Round-nose pliers
- Wire cutters

TECHNIQUES

- Opening and Closing Jump Rings
- Cutting Chain
- Forming a Loop
- Forming a Wrapped Loop

Level:
◈ ◈ ◦

Time:
◈ ◦ ◦

Champagne Woven Earrings

When you need something to pair with a little black dress, look no further than these earrings. Their simple shape and subtle colors make them an elegant piece for any party. Pair them with a sleek ponytail or another simple updo.

1 *Make the first loop.* Cut a 10" (26cm) length of beading wire. String a crimp bead, a 6mm champagne crystal bicone, a crimp bead, a 6mm champagne crystal bicone, a crimp bead, a 6mm champagne crystal bicone, and a crimp bead onto the middle of the wire.

2 *Make the second loop.* Crisscross both ends of the wire through one 6mm champagne crystal bicone. Then string a crimp bead, a 4mm aqua/gold crystal bicone, and a crimp bead onto each end of the wire.

3 *Make the third loop.* Crisscross both ends of the wire through a 4mm aqua/gold crystal bicone. Then string a crimp bead, a 4mm aqua/gold crystal bicone, and a crimp bead onto each end of the wire.

4 *Make the fourth loop.* Crisscross both ends of the wire through a 4mm champagne crystal bicone. Then string a crimp bead, a 4mm champagne crystal bicone, and a crimp bead onto each end of the wire.

5 *Add the last bead.* Crisscross each end of the wire through a 4mm champagne crystal bicone.

6 *Close the earring.* Use a crimp bead to connect both ends of the wire to a 4mm jump ring using a closed loop.

7 *Add the earring wire.* Slide the jump ring onto the open loop on the bottom of a kidney earring wire. Use needle-nose pliers to pinch the open loop together.

8 *Make the other earring.* Repeat Steps 1–7 for the matching earring.

SHOPPING LIST

- 8 - 6mm crystal bicone beads (champagne)
- 8 - 4mm crystal bicone beads (champagne)
- 10 - 4mm crystal bicone beads (AB aqua/gold)
- 34 - Crimp beads (gold)
- 20" (52cm) - Beading wire (gold)
- 2 - 4mm jump rings (gold)
- 2 - Kidney earring wires (gold)

TOOLS

- Needle-nose pliers
- Crimping pliers
- Wire cutters

TECHNIQUES

- Attaching Crimp Tubes/Beads

Frosted Crystal Necklace

Level:
♦♦•

Time:
♦♦•

This necklace will bring a touch of sparkle and shine to any outfit. Wear it with dark clothing to give the crystal and beads center stage, or keep your clothing light for a subtle shimmer. Make your look cohesive with earrings and bracelets in a similar style and a sparkly pair of shoes.

1. *Prepare the wires.* Cut a 22" (56cm), a 21" (53.5cm), and a 20" (51cm) length of beading wire.

2. *String the first wire.* String the following onto the middle of the 22" (56cm) beading wire: 1 crimp tube, 7 bicones, 1 crimp tube, the druzy pendant, 1 crimp tube, 7 bicones, and 1 crimp tube.

3. *String the second wire.* String the following onto the middle of the 21" (53.5cm) beading wire: 1 crimp tube, 13 bicones, and 1 crimp tube. Bring the ends of the 21" (53.5cm) wire up through the crimp tubes on each end of the 22" (56cm) wire from Step 2, then string 4 bicones and 1 crimp tube onto each end of the two joined wires.

4. *String the third wire.* String the following onto the middle of the 20" (51cm) beading wire: 1 crimp tube, 19 bicones, and 1 crimp tube. Bring the ends of the 20" (51cm) wire up through the crimp tubes on each end of the joined wires from Steps 2–3, then string 6½" (16.5cm) of additional bicones (about 45 bicones per side) onto each end of the three joined wires.

5. *Make the extender chain.* Slide 3 bicones onto a head pin and form a loop to make a bead drop. Connect the loop of the bead drop to one end of the extender chain. Attach a 6mm jump ring to the other end of the extender chain. Use a crimp tube to connect the 6mm jump ring to one end of the 3 joined wires.

6. *Add the clasp.* Attach a 4mm jump ring to a lobster clasp. Use a crimp tube to connect a 4mm jump ring to the other end of the 3 joined wires.

SHOPPING LIST

- 1 - 27 x 20mm druzy crystal pendant (white)
- 147 - 4mm crystal bicone beads (AB clear)
- 63" (161cm) - Beading wire (silver)
- 12 - Crimp tubes (silver)
- 1 - 1" (2.5cm) extender chain (silver)
- 1 - 1" (2.5cm) head pin (silver)
- 1 - 6mm jump ring (silver)
- 1 - 4mm jump ring (silver)
- 1 - Lobster clasp (silver)

TOOLS

- Needle-nose pliers
- Round-nose pliers
- Crimping pliers
- Wire cutters

TECHNIQUES

- Opening and Closing Jump Rings
- Attaching Crimp Tubes/Beads
- Forming a Loop

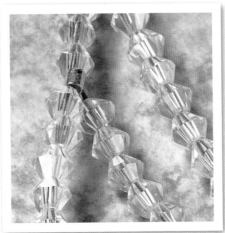

Level:
◆ ◆ ●

Time:
◆ ◆ ●

Beaded Tassel Bracelet Set

These bracelets are classy and chic with a touch of whimsy. Pair them with a sparkly top for a night out with the girls or with your favorite work outfit. Substitute beads in different colors or styles—like bright neons—for a totally new look.

1 **Attach the clasp.** Cut a 12" (30.5cm) length of beading wire. Use a crimp tube to attach one end of the wire directly to a lobster clasp. (Alternatively, you can attach the wire to the lobster clasp using a crimp tube and a 4mm jump ring.)

2 **String the beads.** String on almond pearl beads to desired length. Use a crimp tube to connect the other end of the wire to a 6mm jump ring. Trim excess wire.

3 **Attach the chain.** Cut eleven 1" (2.5cm) lengths of white chain. Slide the first link of each of the chain lengths onto an eye pin and form a loop. Attach the loop to the 6mm jump ring from Step 2.

4 **Make the remaining bracelets.** Repeat Steps 1–3 to make two more bracelets, one with the silver mirror beads and silver chain and one with the black bicones and black chain.

 SHOPPING LIST

- 34 - 6mm round beads (AB silver mirror)
- 34 - 6mm glass bicone beads (black)
- 34 - 6mm glass round beads (almond pearl)
- 25" (64cm) - 2.3 mm curb chain (silver)
- 25" (64cm) - 2.3mm curb chain (black)
- 25" (64cm) - 1.8mm curb chain (white)
- 36" (92cm) - Beading wire (silver)
- 6 - Crimp tubes (silver)
- 3 - 1" (2.5cm) eye pins (silver)
- 3 - 6mm jump rings (silver)
- 3 - Lobster clasps (silver)

TOOLS

- Round-nose pliers
- Crimping pliers
- Wire cutters

TECHNIQUES

- Opening and Closing Jump Rings
- Attaching Crimp Tubes/Beads
- Cutting Chain
- Forming a Loop

Coral Swirl Earrings

With their spiral shape, these earrings give off a fun vibe that's perfect for a night out. You can customize the size of the earrings by using more wire and beads to create a larger spiral or less wire and fewer beads to create a smaller spiral.

1 *Form the earring shape.* Cut a 9" (23cm) length of 20-gauge wire. Coil the wire around the ring mandrel, leaving about 2" (5cm) of wire uncoiled. Remove the wire from the mandrel and flatten into an open, flat spiral shape, beginning with a small coil in the center and ending with a 2" (5cm) tail.

2 *Form the earring wire.* Bend and form the remaining 2" (5cm) of the wire into a large earring wire perpendicular to the spiral so the spiral will face forward on the ear, more or less parallel to the face. Hold it up to your ear to check the direction. Trim excess wire.

3 *Add the beads.* Cut a 24" (61cm) length of 24-gauge wire. Wire wrap a 6/0 E-bead into the middle of the center loop of the spiral. Continue wire wrapping beads onto the outside edge of the coiled wire until you reach the end of the spiral.

4 *Finish wrapping.* Continue wrapping the 24-gauge wire around the 20-gauge wire about ¼" (0.6cm) up the base of the earring wire, then trim excess wire.

5 *Make the other earring.* Repeat Steps 1–4 for the matching earring.

 SHOPPING LIST

- 56 - 6/0 E-beads (champagne)
- 18" (46cm) - 20-gauge wire (gold)
- 48" (122cm) - 24-gauge wire (gold)

TOOLS

- Needle-nose pliers
- Round-nose pliers
- Wire cutters
- Ring mandrel

TECHNIQUES

- Forming Wire Wraps with Beads

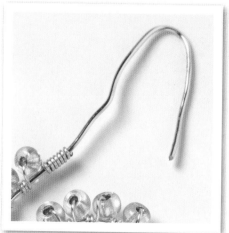

Lariat Layers Necklace Set

Level:
◆ ◆ ●

Time:
◆ ◆ ●

What better way to mix it up than with this versatile necklace set? Wear these two pieces together or separately. The simple designs can go dressy or casual—pair them with a black dress and gold shoes or a t-shirt. For a unique twist, turn the lariat necklace around so the end extends down your back—perfect for scoop-back tops.

SHORT NECKLACE

1 *Prepare the necklace.* Cut an 18" (46cm) length of chain. Use a jump ring to connect a lobster clasp to one end of the chain. Connect another jump ring to the other end of the chain.

2 *Add the drops.* Use jump rings to connect 3 bar drops and 2 rectangle drops to links in the chain as follows: a bar drop in the middle of the chain, then a rectangle and a bar drop to each side of the center drop, skipping 3 chain links between each drop.

LARIAT NECKLACE

1 *Prepare the chain.* Cut a 26" (66cm) and a 1" (2.5cm) length of chain. Use a jump ring to connect a bar drop to each end of the 26" (66cm) chain.

2 *Prepare the first wire.* Cut two 18" (46cm) lengths of 24-gauge wire. Create a wrapped loop on one end of one of the wires.

3 *Wrap the first bar.* Hold the leading edge of wire from the wrapped loop from Step 2 to the back of the bottom end of one of the bar drops from Step 1. Begin wrapping the wire up and around the bar 8–9 times to get the desired wrapped look. To finish the link, wrap the wire 2–3 times around one side of the loop on the bar drop. Trim excess wire.

4 *Add the small chain.* Use a jump ring to connect one end of the 1" (2.5cm) chain to the wrapped loop from Step 2.

5 *Prepare the second wire.* Create a wrapped loop on one end of the second wire from Step 2, attaching the circle half of the toggle clasp to it.

6 *Wrap the second bar.* Repeat the process used in Step 3 using the wire from Step 5 to wrap the remaining bar drop.

7 *Connect the pieces.* Use a jump ring to connect the other end of the 1" (2.5cm) chain to the top of the bar drop from Step 6.

SHOPPING LIST

- 6 - 22 x 2mm bar drops (matte gold)
- 2 - 28 x 6mm rectangle drops (matte gold)
- 36" (92cm) - 24-gauge wire (gold)
- 46" (117cm) - 1.8mm curb chain (gold)
- 11 - 4mm jump rings (gold)
- 1 - 12mm toggle clasp set (matte gold)
- 1 - Lobster clasp (gold)

TOOLS

- Needle-nose pliers
- Round-nose pliers
- Wire cutters

TECHNIQUES

- Opening and Closing Jump Rings
- Forming a Wrapped Loop
- Wrapping Beads with Wire

Silver Bubbles Earrings

Level:
◈◈◦

Time:
◈◦◦

With a pack of jump rings and some earring wires, you can fashion yourself a beautiful set of earrings at a bargain price. This design is fun and flirty with lots of movement, making it a great pick for a night out, but they won't look out of place at a dinner party either!

1 *Make the central chain.* Connect eighteen 4mm jump rings together in a row to make a jump ring chain.

2 *Add the earring wire.* Connect a jump ring from one end of the chain to the bottom loop of an earring wire so the jump ring chain hangs down from the earring wire.

3 *Add the large jump rings.* Add two 8mm jump rings to each of the top 2 jump rings in the jump ring chain, 1 on each side of the center.

4 *Add the medium jump rings.* Add two 6mm jump rings to each of the next 7 jump rings down in the jump ring chain, 1 on each side of the center.

5 *Add the small jump rings.* Add two 4mm jump rings to each of the next 7 jump rings down in the jump ring chain, 1 on each side of the center. This will leave the bottom 2 central jump rings unadorned.

6 *Make the other earring.* Repeat Steps 1–5 for the matching earring.

SHOPPING LIST

- 64 - 4mm jump rings (silver)
- 28 - 6mm jump rings (silver)
- 8 - 8mm jump rings (silver)
- 2 - Earring wires (silver)

TOOLS

- Needle-nose pliers

TECHNIQUES

- Opening and Closing Jump Rings

Level:
♦♦•

Time:
♦♦•

Evening Elegance Necklace

With its layered chains and wide variety of beads, this necklace is the perfect way to dress up a simple outfit. Pair it with a chic dress, a tailored work outfit, or your favorite skinny jeans and heels. Don't forget a set of simple gold bangles!

1 **Create the bead drops.** Slide a rhinestone round bead onto a head pin and form a loop. Repeat to make a total of 18 bead drops.

2 **Make the first strand.** Cut a 32" (81.5cm) length of fine curb chain. Find the middle of the chain. Connect a rhinestone bead drop ¾" (2cm) from the middle of the chain on each side. Continue by connecting 8 rhinestone bead drops on each side of the chain every 1½" (3.8cm) past the first two bead drops.

3 **Make the second strand.** Add 4mm jump rings to the holes on each side of the 17 flat round champagne connectors. Cut eighteen 1" (2.5cm) lengths of ball link chain with a gold round in the middle of each length. Starting and ending with a 1" (2.5cm) length of chain, attach a connector between each 1" (2.5cm) chain.

4 **Make the third strand.** Cut a 24" (61cm) length of fine curb chain.

5 **Make the fourth strand.** Add a 4mm jump ring to each side of 8 tan/gold oval connectors. Cut nine 1¼" (3.2cm) lengths of cable chain. Starting and ending with a 1¼" (3.2cm) length of chain, attach a connector between each 1¼" (3.2cm) chain.

6 **Connect the strands.** Use a 6mm gold jump ring to connect one side of the 4 necklace strands together, in order with the first strand at the bottom and the fourth strand at the top. Repeat on the other side of the strands.

7 **Finish the necklace.** Connect another 6mm jump ring to the existing 6mm jump ring on each side of the necklace. Add the decorative S-hook connector to the last 6mm jump ring on one side of the necklace, and the 8mm closed jump ring to the other.

 SHOPPING LIST

- 18 - 6mm rhinestone round beads (gold/clear)
- 17 - 12mm flat round acrylic connectors (champagne)
- 8 - 18 x 10mm flat oval connectors (tan/gold)
- 56" (145cm) - 2mm curb chain (gold)
- 28" (72cm) - 1.8mm cable chain with 3mm round beads (gold)
- 16" (41cm) - 4mm cable chain (gold)
- 18 - 1" (2.5cm) ball head pins (gold)
- 50 - 4mm jump rings (gold)
- 4 - 6mm jump rings (gold)
- 1 - 8mm closed jump ring (gold)
- 1 - 22 x 8mm decorative S-hook clasp (gold)

TOOLS

- Needle-nose pliers (2 pairs)
- Round-nose pliers
- Wire cutters

TECHNIQUES

- Opening and Closing Jump Rings
- Cutting Chain
- Forming a Loop

Clear Skies Beaded Earrings

Loads of bead drops give these earrings loads of fun movement! Change up the look by substituting the blue beads for another color. Blue is carefree and airy; orange, red, or pink beads will be bright and exciting; and black beads will be chic and elegant.

1 *Add the chain.* Cut a 4-link length of chain. Use a jump ring to attach one end of the chain to the bottom middle of an earring hoop.

2 *Add the central bead.* Slide a teardrop onto a ball head pin. Form a wrapped loop with the ball head pin to connect this bead drop to the bottom link of the 4-link chain.

3 *Add the cluster beads.* Slide a bicone onto a ball head pin. Form a wrapped loop with the ball head pin to connect this bead drop to the second link up of the 4-link chain. Repeat to connect bead drops as follows: 1 to the other side of the second link up on the chain, 1 on each side of the third link up on the chain, 1 on each side of the top link of the chain, and 1 to the jump ring connecting the top of the chain to the earring hoop. This will total 7 bead drops added to the central bead strand.

4 *Make bead drops.* Slide a bicone onto a ball head pin and form a wrapped loop just large enough to slide onto the earring hoop. Repeat to make a total of 10 bead drops.

5 *Add bead drops.* Slide the loops of 5 bead drops onto each side of the earring hoop so the cluster from Step 3 hangs in the middle. Close the wire at the top of the earring hoop. Connect the loop of an earring wire to the top of the earring hoop.

6 *Make the other earring.* Repeat Steps 1–5 for the matching earring.

SHOPPING LIST

- 2 - 10 x 8mm crystal teardrops (champagne)
- 34 - 4mm crystal bicone beads (aqua)
- 2" (5cm) - 2mm curb chain (gold)
- 36 - 1" (2.5cm) ball head pins (gold)
- 2 - 4mm jump rings (gold)
- 2 - 21mm earring hoops (gold)
- 2 - 13mm ball hook earring wires (gold)

TOOLS

- Needle-nose pliers
- Round-nose pliers
- Wire cutters

TECHNIQUES

- Opening and Closing Jump Rings
- Forming a Wrapped Loop

Starlight Shimmer Necklace

This project uses just a few components—chain, jump rings, and a clasp—to create a gorgeously complex chain mail effect. You'll be thrilled with the end result! The simple design makes this a great go-to piece for any occasion. Swap out the silver components for gold, if you prefer.

Before You Begin: Refer to the diagram while following Steps 1–4, but use two 6mm jump rings at a time instead of just one 6mm jump ring—called jump ring "duos" and given letter designations A–I to help remind you.

1   *Prepare the center.* Attach six 4mm jump rings to a 6mm jump ring duo (A).

2   *Start the center rows.* Attach a 6mm jump ring duo (B, C, D, E, F, G) to each 4mm jump ring from Step 1. Lay this arrangement of 6 jump ring duos surrounding a seventh jump ring duo flat. It should roughly form a flower shape.

3   *Connect the center rows.* Use 6 sets of two 4mm jump rings to connect each of the 6 outer jump ring duos (B, C, D, E, F, G) together in a circle, and lay this arrangement flat. You should still see the flower shape, but it should be secured in place by the 4mm jump rings.

4   *Add the top and bottom.* Take a jump ring duo (H) and use 1 set of two 4mm jump rings to connect it to the jump ring duo C and 1 set of two 4mm jump rings to connect it to the jump ring duo D. Repeat to attach the remaining jump ring duo (I) to jump ring duos G and F. Lay this arrangement flat. You should now have a diamond shape that matches the diagram.

5   *Make the tassel.* Cut one 18" (46cm) and six 2½" (6.5cm) lengths of chain. Connect one end of each 2½" (6.5cm) length of chain to a single 4mm jump ring. Use another 4mm jump ring to connect that jump ring to the single 6mm jump ring duo at the bottom of the diamond from Step 4 (I).

6   *Attach the chain.* Connect a 4mm jump ring to the single 6mm jump ring duo at the top of the diamond from Step 4 (H). Thread the 18" (46cm) chain through the 4mm jump ring.

7   *Add the clasp.* Use a 4mm jump ring to connect a lobster clasp to one end of the 18" (46cm) chain, and connect another 4mm jump ring to the other end of the 18" (46cm) chain.

SHOPPING LIST

- 36" (92cm) - 1.8mm cable chain (silver)
- 31 - 4mm jump rings (silver)
- 18 - 6mm jump rings (silver)
- 1 - Lobster clasp (silver)

TOOLS

- Needle-nose pliers
- Wire cutters

TECHNIQUES

- Opening and Closing Jump Rings
- Cutting Chain

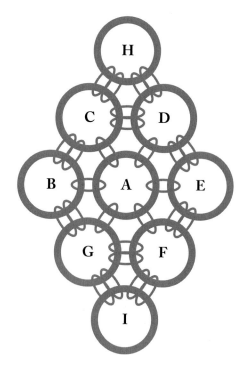

Tip: If you aren't happy with the way your jump rings are laying, try adding an extra jump ring or two to help it keep its shape (as shown in the photos).

Gold Leaf Chain Earrings

This design draws from nature to create a beautiful set of statement earrings. They take a little concentration to make, but the result is stunning! Highlight these earrings with a sleek outfit like tailored pants and a blouse or a sheath dress.

1   *Cut the chain.* Cut the following lengths of chain: six 7-link lengths, eight 8-link lengths, and ten 9-link lengths.

2   *Make the frame.* Cut a 7" (18cm) length of wire. Fold the wire in the middle. Thread the loop of an eye pin onto the fold. On each side of the eye pin, form the wire into a leaf shape.

3   *Start adding beads and 7-link chains.* Slide the following onto the wire on the right and left sides of the leaf: 1 seed bead and one end of a 7-link chain. Slide the following onto the eye pin: 8 seed beads and the other ends of the 7-link chains, first from the right side, then from the left side.

4   *Continue adding beads and 7-link chains.* Slide the following onto the wire on the right and left sides of the leaf: 2 seed beads and one end of a 7-link chain. Side the following onto the eye pin: 1 seed bead and the other ends of the 7-link chains, first from the right side, then from the left side.

5   *Start adding beads and 8-link chains.* Slide the following onto the wire on the right and left sides of the leaf: 2 seed beads and one end of an 8-link chain. Slide the following onto the eye pin: 1 seed bead and the other ends of the 8-link chains, first from the right side, then from the left side.

6   *Repeat Step 5.* Repeat Step 5 two more times.

7   *Start adding beads and 9-link chains.* Slide the following onto the wire on the right and left sides of the leaf: 2 seed beads and one end of a 9-link chain. Slide the following onto the eye pin: 1 seed bead and the other ends of the 9-link chains, first from the right side, then from the left side.

8   *Repeat Step 7.* Repeat Step 7 four more times.

9   *Repeat Step 5.* Repeat Step 5 one more time.

10   *Repeat Step 4.* Repeat Step 4 one more time.

SHOPPING LIST

- 170 - 11/0 glass seed beads (light gold)
- 34" (87cm) - 1.8mm curb chain (gold)
- 14" (36cm) - 24-gauge wire (gold)
- 2 - 2" (5cm) eye pins (gold)
- 2 - Earring wires (gold)

TOOLS

- Needle-nose pliers
- Round-nose pliers
- Wire cutters

TECHNIQUES

- Cutting Chain
- Forming a Loop
- Forming a Wrapped Loop

11 *Finish the core.* Form a loop in the eye pin just after the last chain from Step 10. Trim excess wire.

12 *Finish the edges.* Slide 10 seed beads onto the wire on the right and left sides of the leaf, then form wrapped loops, one on each side of the leaf, that connect to the loop of the eye pin from Step 11. Trim excess wire.

13 *Add the earring wire.* Attach the loop of an earring wire to the top loop of the eye pin.

14 *Make the other earring.* Repeat Steps 1–13 for the matching earring.

Tip: The number of crystal bicones needed and the lengths of the beaded bicone strands may vary depending on the particular textured chain that is used. The length of the chain and the number of beads can also be adjusted for different wrist sizes.

Chain-Link Crystal Bracelet

Level:
♦ ♦ ♦

Time:
♦ ♦ •

If you like a lot of bling, you'll love showing off this bracelet. Use it to dress up a casual outfit, or pair it with a showstopping ensemble for a night out. Match your style by changing up the color of the beads to make a design that's unique to you.

1 *Attach the closure.* Attach two 6mm jump rings to the links on each end of the textured chain. Use a single 6mm jump ring to attach a lobster clasp to one set of 2 jump rings. Use another 6mm jump ring to attach an extender chain to the other set of 2 jump rings.

2 *Add the bead drop.* Slide a topaz bicone onto a head pin. Form a wrapped loop with the head pin to attach the bead drop to the end of the extender chain.

3 *Prepare the wires.* Cut two 12" (30.5cm) lengths of beading wire. Use crimp tubes to attach one end of each wire to one of the 6mm jump rings at one end of the chain (one wire per jump ring).

4 *Bead the wires.* Alternating the colors as you go, string 49 bicones onto one beading wire and 59 bicones onto the other beading wire.

5 *Finish the beaded wires.* String on a crimp tube just beyond the last bicone on each beading wire. Bring the wires back through the crimp tubes, leaving a small loop on each just large enough to slide onto a jump ring. Close the crimp tube and trim excess wire.

6 *Weave the beaded wires.* Alternating sides, weave the bicone strands back and forth through the textured chain links until you reach the other end of the bracelet. Open the 2 jump rings attached to the textured chain on that end of the bracelet. Connect the tiny loops at the end of the beaded wires to the jump rings. Securely close the jump rings.

SHOPPING LIST

- 27 - 4mm crystal bicone beads (topaz)
- 27 - 4mm crystal bicone beads (light yellow)
- 27 - 4mm crystal bicone beads (light amethyst)
- 27 - 4mm crystal bicone beads (clear)
- 7" (18cm) - 19 x 8mm textured chain (silver)
- 24" (61cm) - Beading wire (silver)
- 4 - Crimp tubes (silver)
- 1 - 2" (5cm) extender chain (silver)
- 1 - 1" (2.5cm) head pin (silver)
- 6 - 6mm jump rings (silver)
- 1 - Lobster clasp (silver)

TOOLS

- Needle-nose pliers
- Round-nose pliers
- Crimping pliers
- Wire cutters

TECHNIQUES

- Opening and Closing Jump Rings
- Attaching Crimp Tubes/Beads
- Forming a Wrapped Loop

Gold Wrap Crystal Earrings

These earrings are made with classic materials, but have a funky, modern design that gives them a unique twist. Give this design a pop of color by substituting the clear beads for ones in your favorite shade, or try silver findings instead of gold.

1. *Make the frame.* Cut a 10" (25.5cm) length of 20-gauge wire. Form a wrapped loop at one end of the wire, then form a rectangle that is about 1⅞" (4.8cm) long and ⅜" (1cm) wide. Wrap the end of the wire back around the wrapped loop at the top of the rectangle. Trim excess wire. Use the hammer to flatten the wire frame. Hammer one side flat, then flip it over to hammer the other side. Use a surface that can handle the impact of hammering, like a workbench or a bench block.

2. *Add the beads.* Cut a 10" (25.5cm) length of 24-gauge wire. Wrap one end around the bottom of the rectangle 3 times. String on 10 bicones with the wire leading up toward the top of the rectangle, centered in the frame. Wrap the end of the wire around the loop at the top of the rectangle and trim excess wire.

3. *Wrap the frame.* Cut a 20" (51cm) length of 24-gauge wire. Wrap one end around the bottom of the rectangle 3 times. Wrap the wire up and around the entire rectangle frame, between each bicone. When you reach the top, wrap the end of the wire around the loop at the top of the rectangle and trim excess wire.

4. *Add the earring wire.* Connect the top loop of the rectangle to the bottom of an earring wire.

5. *Make the other earring.* Repeat Steps 1–4 for the matching earring.

🛍 SHOPPING LIST

- 20 - 4mm crystal bicone beads (clear)
- 20" (51cm) - 20-gauge wire (gold)
- 60" (155cm) - 24-gauge wire (gold)
- 2 - Earring wires (gold)

TOOLS

- Needle-nose pliers
- Round-nose pliers
- Wire cutters
- Jewelry hammer

TECHNIQUES

- Opening and Closing Jump Rings
- Forming a Wrapped Loop
- Wrapping Beads with Wire

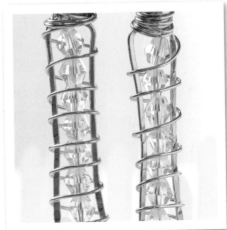

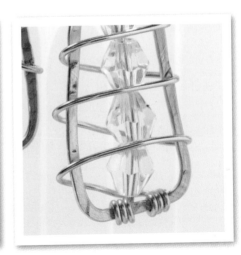

GLOSSARY

Here are a few more miscellaneous terms you might encounter in the Shopping Lists in this book and in the jewelry aisles at your local craft store. For the definitions of most other tools and materials mentioned in this book, see pages 10–13.

Miscellaneous Terms

AB: standing for "aurora borealis," a type of bead finish applied to one side of the bead that reflects different iridescent colors.

druzy crystal: a stone with many tiny, fine crystals on top of a colorful mineral. They are very sparkly and colorful.

extender chain: a short length of chain used at the clasp to make the size of a jewelry piece flexible.

lariat: a necklace style that has a long, straight drop coming from the middle of the necklace. This type of necklace usually does not have a clasp.

Key Types of Chain

cable chain: chain that has interlocking links that are either round or oval in shape.

curb chain: chain that has interlocking links that are semi-curved and seem to interlock on an angle, allowing the chain to lie flat.

flat-link chain: any chain that has interlocking links where each link is somewhat flattened on its sides.

double-link chain: any chain that has two links paired up in place of single links.

drawn cable chain: cable chain with links that are stretched/elongated.

rope chain: chain that has multiple layers of links connected in a spiral-esque pattern, creating a rope effect.

figure-8 chain: chain that has figure-8 shaped links.

Features of Key Materials for Beads/Pendants

glass: very widely available, cheap to expensive, many different cuts and shapes.

crystal: widely available, cheap to expensive.

acrylic: widely available, affordable.

resin: less widely available, affordable.

gemstone: widely available, affordable to expensive, heavy weight.

INDEX